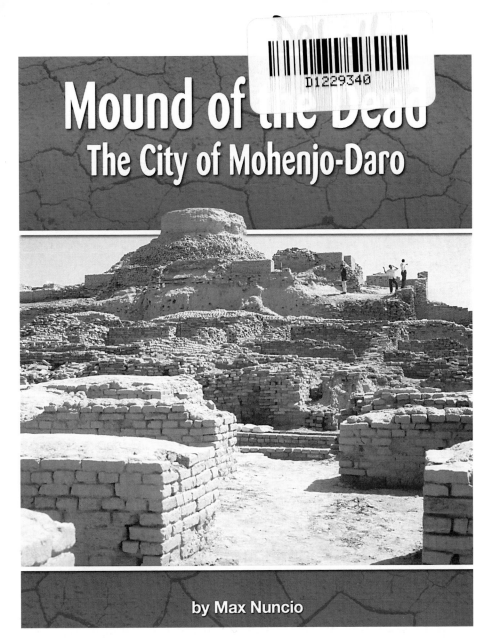

Mound of the Dead
The City of Mohenjo-Daro

by Max Nuncio

HOUGHTON MIFFLIN   BOSTON

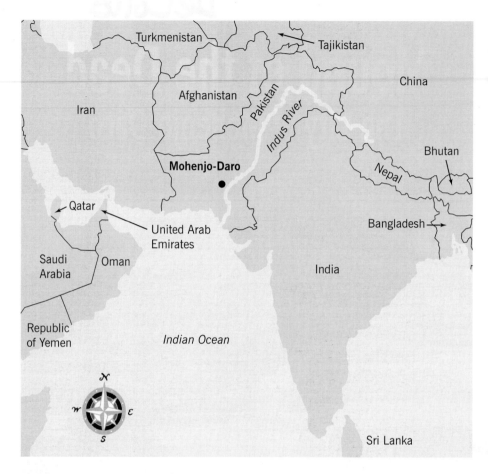

Mohenjo-Daro, Pakistan

Mohenjo-Daro: Mound of the Dead

You are traveling along beside an old farm field in southwest Pakistan. A blistering sun glints off the hard, dry land. The truck bounces over ruts. A cloud of dust billows behind you. You can see for miles across the flat landscape. In the distance you see a mound; or is it a hill? A mirage? As you approach, you see something totally unexpected. Brick walls and a tower become visible. Streets and buildings appear. The mound turns out to be a city. A silent city. It is Mohenjo-Daro, known as the Mound of the Dead. It is very, very old.

Three Ancient Civilizations

About 5,000 years ago, people developed written language. They began to make signs and pictures that stood for things. Sometimes a picture stood for an idea. Sometimes a picture stood for a sound. The pictures developed into alphabet letters.

Archaelogical site of the Indus Valley

Fields of buckwheat in the Indus Valley, Ladakh, India

During this time, civilizations emerged. The civilizations were made up of many villages. One ruler or ruling group led all of the villages. Eventually, one or two villages grew into cities. The ruler built palaces and temples in the city. Three great civilizations developed: Sumerian, Egyptian, and Indus Valley.

The Sumerian people lived in the valley between the Euphrates and Tigris Rivers. By 5,000 years ago, they had an alphabet for their language. They recorded their knowledge and history. They built libraries. They also built tall towers, which they used for worshiping their gods. The remains of the towers can still be seen today. The Sumerians left behind evidence of war and conquest.

Egyptian civilization grew up along the Nile River. You've probably seen pictures of the monuments the Egyptians left behind — the great pyramids. The pyramids were tombs for Egypt's kings. The Egyptians believed that their kings were gods. The kings directed every aspect of Egyptian life. The Egyptians developed a picture-writing system. They, too, built libraries filled with books on science, history, and religion. The Egyptians were also fighters.

The third civilization of 5,000 years ago was the civilization that built Mohenjo-Daro. It also developed along a river valley — the Indus River Valley in today's Pakistan. The Indus Valley people also developed an alphabet. They built large cities. But the people of the Indus Valley were not warlike. Few weapons have been found from their time. They also did not build temples or tombs. Their religious life seems to have been quiet.

Indus Valley Life

The Indus Valley civilization prospered from about 2500 B.C.E. until about 1700 B.C.E. Mohenjo-Daro was inhabited during much of that time. The civilization controlled an area much larger than early Egypt or Sumeria. Its territory was twice the size of Texas.

The Indus Valley people were business people and traders. They brought raw materials from mountain villages north of the Indus River to the river valley cities. In cities such as Mohenjo-Daro, artists made items with the raw materials. They made jewelry, beads, and pottery. They wove cloth. Indus people also brought finished goods from the mountain villages.

Merchants took the finished goods — whether village-made or city-made — along the Indus River and the rivers that flowed into it. They sailed on Indus River Valley ships to other cities and traded with the people there. For example, beads made in the Indus Valley have been found in Sumerian and Egyptian tombs. Four or five Indus Valley cities grew larger than the others. They became capital cities of the empire. Harappa, Lothal, and Mohenjo-Daro are the three best-known capital cities. They were all built using similar materials and methods. All three looked very much alike.

Mound of the Dead — or Not?

The ruins of Mohenjo-Daro were discovered in the 1920s. Several digs have been made there. During a dig, archeologists remove soil that has built up over a place. On the first dig, archeologists found several skeletons. The scientists thought that the mound must have been a burial ground. That's why they called it Mohenjo-Daro. *Mohenjo* means "dead" in Hindi.

Daro means "mound." Hindi was the main language spoken by the archeologists.

People working on later digs found no more skeletons at the Mound of the Dead. It turned out to be very much a city of the living. Mohenjo-Daro is large. It would take someone at least an hour to walk around the three-mile city boundary.

The ruins of Harappa, Pakistan, northeast of Mohenjo-Daro

It is a city of right angles. The main city is made up of two rectangles. Each rectangle is then divided into other rectangles and squares.

The city is carefully oriented, too. The sides of the squares and rectangles point directly north, south, east, or west. The city was built skillfully using this plan. Harappa and Lothal are laid out in the same way.

Bricks

Mohenjo-daro is built of bricks. Brick-making was important. Bricks can be made in two ways. The first way is to make a wet mud mixture. Then the mud is shaped into bricks and left to dry. The second way starts the same. After shaping mud into bricks and left to dry, the workers heat the bricks. Then they fire, or bake, the bricks, as in pottery making.

Mud bricks can be made quickly. They are also easily unmade. A heavy rain will begin to wash them away. Fired bricks are strong. They last through fire and flood. They last for centuries. The fired bricks at Mohenjo-Daro have lasted for 30 centuries.

At Harappa, many of the ancient fired bricks were stolen and used for homes. In the 1800s, many bricks from Harappa were used to build a railroad bed. Archeologists wince at the damage. The removal of the bricks makes it hard to know what Harappa was like. But it does show how strong the bricks were.

The Indus people probably used fired bricks because of flooding. In that part of the world, heavy rains, called

The Great Bath at Mohenjo-Daro was made of bricks.

monsoons, come through once a year. The Indus River rises above its banks. Homes and roads are washed away. Mud bricks could not have survived the annual rain. City workers would have had to rebuild Mohenjo-Daro every year if mud bricks were used. Today, the Indus River's course has changed. It no longer flows near the city.

The Citadel

The round building seen today in pictures of Mohenjo-Daro is not part of the ancient city. It is a Buddhist temple built many centuries later. The priests built it on the highest land around — the ruins of Mohenjo-Daro. They built the temple on Mohenjo-Daro's Citadel. A citadel is a city walled against invaders.

The first archeologists to dig at the site named it. Again, they made a mistake. They thought that the strong brick walls they found must have been used to protect a castle. The high part of the ruins would be the best place to guard against enemies. So they named it the Citadel. But no evidence of weapons or war has ever been found near the city. It is more likely that the walls were built strongly to protect against high water.

The Citadel is the upper rectangle of Mohenjo-Daro. It holds what is probably the world's first swimming pool. A huge square basin is lined to make it waterproof. Steps lead down into it. Drainage tunnels lead away from the pool. A two-story building originally surrounded it.

No one knows what the pool was for. Bathing may have been an important part of the Indus Valley religion. On the other hand, the pool may have been for recreation. But its position in the center of the Citadel shows that whatever happened there was very important to the life of the city.

The Citadel also has a large building called the Granary. It was a warehouse for grains. Long aisles of raised shelves held pottery jars full of wheat and rice. A wooden roof (long since rotted away) kept the grain dry. One end of the Granary opened onto a dock on the Indus River. Grain was loaded and unloaded there.

The Citadel at Mohenjo-Daro, c. 200 A.D.

Grain was important for other reasons besides its value as food. Grain was used as money at Mohenjo-Daro. Those who did a service for the government were paid with grain. When people needed to buy something, they paid for it in grain. All of the larger Indus cities being uncovered have some sort of granary.

The Citadel has large meeting halls whose roofs were held up by posts. It also has a building made up of many small rooms, almost as in a dormitory or an apartment building. Each "apartment" had two rooms. The larger inner room was probably a sleeping room. The outer smaller room was a bathroom.

City with Indoor Plumbing

The lower rectangle of Mohenjo-Daro is called the lower city. The lower city contained mostly houses. Main streets were wide. They intersected each other at right angles. Smaller streets branched off from the main streets.

Even though the streets were lined with houses, there were no windows facing the street. The houses were built around courtyards. Windows overlooked the courtyards. Small houses had at least three rooms. Larger houses had more rooms. Most houses had stairs leading up to what must have been a second floor. The upper story may have been built of wood. That would explain why there are no walls left on the upper story. However, since the weather was hot and dry much of the year, perhaps the upper story was simply a roof patio.

A stone staircase in the ancient Indus Valley civilization

One thing is known for sure. The people of Mohenjo-Daro had indoor toilets. Neither the Egyptians nor the Sumerians had indoor plumbing. Most people did not have it until the 1900s. The Indus Valley people were ahead of their time.

Cleanliness was very important to the Indus Valley people. One of the rooms in each house was a bathroom with indoor plumbing. People bathed there and took showers by pouring water over their heads. A floor drain took the water out of the house.

Likewise, waste left the house through a pipe. The drains and pipes emptied into a sewer that ran down the length of the streets. To keep the streets clean, the Indus people covered the sewer with large stones. The wastewater was taken out of town. It may have been used as fertilizer in the fields outside of the city. The homes in Harappa and Lothal also had indoor plumbing.

The Seals of Mohenjo-Daro

Structures made of fired bricks have lasted. For instance, the plumbing in Mohenjo-Daro is lined with fired bricks. Items of stone and metal also remain. Most of the metal objects are jewelry. The metal in the jewelry is interlaced with stone or clay beads. A special kind of bead called carnelian turned red when it was fired.

But stone seals best represent the people of the Indus Valley. The seals are made from a kind of soapstone. Soapstone is easily carved. The seals were small cubes of soapstone, about one inch on a side.

The people of Mohenjo-Daro used seals to mark their property. They pressed the carved end of the seal into soft clay. The impression left by the seal then hardened into the clay.

One face of the cube had a drawing carved into it. The drawings were most often animals. People and fantasy animals